Love like GOD

Companion Book

Further Explorations of Unconditional Love

Love

like

GOD

Companion Book

Further Explorations of Unconditional Love

Caroline A. Shearer

Absolute Love Publishing

Absolute Love Publishing

Love Like God
Companion Book

Published by
Absolute Love Publishing
USA

Cover design by Sarah Picciuto

Cover artwork © Jenny Speckels. Original abstract painting of an opening flower releasing white light. Inspired by the "Flower of Creation"

Cover headshot by Prabhakar Gopalan

ISBN:
978-0-9833017-1-4

Printed in the United States of America

For the Seekers

Contents

"Your task is not to seek for love,
but merely to seek and find all the barriers
within yourself that you have built against it."

- Rumi

How to Use This Book

It is my belief that to truly absorb a concept, we need to contemplate the subject matter – and then allow ourselves the space to incorporate it into our structure of reality.

This is the idea with the "Love Like God Companion Book." Basic constructs of absolute love are placed at the beginning of the book, followed by Thoughts, Affirmations, and Love in Action Steps. Some may want to read these straight through and then re-read them at a slower pace; others may want to meditate on one Thought and one Affirmation per day or per week. It's important for readers to choose what works best for themselves, in order to begin fully incorporating these concepts and practices.

I also encourage readers to return over and over to "My Philosophy on Unconditional Love," presented later in this book. Reading these statements will help "ground" readers in these fundamentals as they move forward in their practice of unconditional love.

Preface

This book is a companion to "Love Like God: Embracing Unconditional Love" by bestselling author Caroline A. Shearer.

"Love Like God" is a compilation book created by Absolute Love Publishing that helps us form an awareness of how we, through our life experiences, can love like God. It features almost 40 stories from well-known individuals who share the experiences that helped them learn to release conditions on love. It was created with the intention of inspiring readers to open their own hearts to these possibilities, through understanding how others have begun their journeys toward absolute (unconditional) love.

The original contributors include: Portia Berry Allen (Lady Rerun,) K.L. and Tiffany Braxton Belvin, Jesse Birkey, Chase Block, Anicia Bragg, Kundan Chhabra, Robin Craig, Crystal Dwyer, Tonya Fitzpatrick, Esq., Vida Ghaffari, Lisa Gibson, Jon Graves, Gayle Gregory, Diana Y. Harris, Dana Heidkamp, Jennifer Hicks, Jennifer K. Hunt, Dr. Matthew B. James, Jacquie Jordan, Dr. Judy Kuriansky, Lori La Bey, Sharmen Lane, Nicole Lanning, Rick Lannoye, Katharine C. McCorkle, Ph.D., Shirley W. Mitchell, Kristen Moeller, Roy Nelson, Paramahamsa Nithyananda (Life Bliss Swami,) Deva Premal, Claudio Reilsono, Dea Shandera and Brent N. Hunter, Lorelei Shellist, Dr. Joseph Shrand, Leesa Sklover, Ph.D., Cliff Snider, Laura Stinchfield, Gloria Tom Wing Staudt, Tom Von Deck, and Tom Wright.

You may recognize many of these names. The touching stories from these luminaries include learning to love through addiction, cancer, terrorism, self-doubt, widowhood, romantic relationships, family relationships, pet relationships, and more. We highly encourage you to read their stories and learn more about them in the original book, "Love Like God," and to treat this companion as a philosophical addition to your journey.

This companion features the "Thoughts from Caroline" and the "Affirmations" that accompany each essay in "Love Like God." It also includes further reflections from the author and "Love in Action Steps." It is intended to be a supplement to the original book, to introduce new readers to absolute love, and to help readers focus on specific areas in which they wish to release conditions on love.

You are wished much success and much joy on your journey. As each of us releases a condition on love so then does the world begin to reflect this consciousness. May we all move forward to the freedom of absolute love.

What Unconditional Love Means for Us

I find most people welcome the idea of unconditional love. People think it sounds wonderful and want to share in this miraculous kind of acceptance. "Let's go love!" they say. But, one moment away, they will admit unconditional love is just an ideal, that we can't possibly love unconditionally in practice.

The human, earthly part of me would tend to agree. Right now, I don't think the vast majority of us are capable of unconditionally loving everyone, all of the time. However, my soul knows we can, and I choose to focus my thoughts and my heart on the ultimate reality of everyone loving absolutely, in every moment.

A fully-filled heart does not have room for fear or for pain. Because absolute love is a return to our true nature, it is a state where fear does not exist, a place where our souls are truly blissful. Imagine that - bliss! All the time, in every moment!

Absolute love begins with a shift in our thoughts. These thought patterns will then begin to manifest more and more often in our actions.

These actions will fulfill us in inspiring ways and will inspire others to begin to think and act unconditionally.

Ultimately, a critical mass will be reached when humankind experiences spontaneous outpourings of unconditional love. Suddenly, as if by magic, the world will see itself through these new lenses of unconditional love!

We will get there when we all believe it is possible.

"Love Like God" and "Love Like God Companion Book" set the stage for this change in consciousness.

Absolute Love versus Unconditional Love

The word "love" should, in principle, need no added description. Love IS absolute, selfless, and complete without condition, attachment, judgement, or fear. Unfortunately, as a society, we have added connotations to the word "love" so that it has begun to represent so much more (and truly, so much less.)

We have fallen away from the meaning of love.

Here is why I use "absolute love":

Using energetic principles, I understand that our reality manifests from our emphasis. When I first decided to share a message of unconditional love for all, I realized this phrasing still put energy into the conditions we place on love. Meaning, on an energetic level, we are still creating the conditions, rather than the love. This led me to look for a word implying a positive meaning, and I found it in "absolute."

Thus, when we use the term "absolute love," we are focusing on the strengths of love – which is where we gain our ability to act and live in love – and to be love.

For the purposes of this book, I use the terms "absolute love" and "unconditional love" interchangeably. I prefer absolute love, but I recognize most people are more familiar with the concept of unconditional love and that this referencing may help them grasp these ideas more deeply.

Hopefully, one day, the world will begin again to equate the word "love" with what it truly means, but, for now, we begin the journey of rediscovering our natural state of absolute love.

Returning to Our Natural State

At birth, we look upon the world with pure love. Our eyes and our hearts offer absolute love for everyone and everything. We completely love ourselves. The world is perfect, and we are perfect beings within that world. Every person we meet is another person for us to love.

We do not know any lesser constructs, such as to doubt or distrust or judge.

But, as we grow, we see others acting fearful and angry and sad. We are taught that protecting ourselves is a "normal" behavior. When we mature, we recognize that people place condition after condition on others and on themselves. We see that the way our soul in heaven offers love is not how people on Earth offer love.

And we learn to adjust.

The light in our eyes begins to fade, and we restrict our perception to see the world through others' eyes. Fear enters our consciousness, and what once was pure love is diluted to a measured and controlled love, tempered by others first proving themselves. Are they safe or worthy? Are we safe or worthy? This is the atrophied state of love in which most of us will embark on our journey to rediscover our true selves.

What if it is possible to return to our natural state of pure love? What if we realize that we have power in the choice? Most importantly, what if we recognize that the yearning inside ourselves to love and be loved absolutely is the inherent and rightful call of our true selves?

It is time to free ourselves from the constraints of the fear-based love we have been taught to equate with actual love. It is time to return to our natural state of absolute love.

Thankfully, if you are reading this book, your mind already has opened, of its own accord, to the possibility that there is something more ...

Why Do We Want to Love Unconditionally?

Why should we want to love absolutely? Why is loving with conditions not enough?

It is because loving with conditions isn't really loving.

Conditional love lacks purity, and it lacks a complete truth. It is, in its essence, not love. It can be affection or loyalty or devotion – and there may be moments when love shines through – but it is not love.

If we say, "I will love you through all these situations – this great one, this bad one, this awful one – but, you know, there is this one thing ... I can't love you through that." It's like saying, "You're almost worth it."

We want to offer unconditional love because that is what we yearn to receive. Love – pure love - is the true food of our souls. It is the defining matter of our existence. We exist not because we love but because we are love.

Giving and receiving absolute love work together. We must allow ourselves to be open to the giving and the receiving of absolute love in order to fully attain either. For most of us, this is a process, but when we choose in each moment to be brave in love, our hearts consistently grow in this direction.

Unconditionally loving includes loving ourselves without expectation and without a need to be a certain way or do certain things. There is no "proving" of ourselves. We are loveable as we are, simply for existing. Many times, it is ourselves we claim to be "almost worth it," and this is perhaps the biggest growth lesson in allowing love.

We can always choose to evolve our souls, but we can do so while continuing to love ourselves absolutely.

Also, when we believe in God or in a Divine presence, we want to unconditionally love to follow His example. After all, who better to emulate than God?

Where Do We Begin?

The wonderful news is that by picking up this book you already have started on a path to absolute love! Like a beam of light into your consciousness, it will shine deeper and brighter with each moment of desire for true love. This is a kind of light that cannot be dampened, for it is our light back home.

Cheer yourself for being brave enough to begin this journey!

Moving to Love

Once we have opened our eyes and our hearts to the concept of unconditional love, we can begin to put it into practice. In my experience, the process follows several steps:

1. Wondering what the word "love" really means and wondering if we are practicing it. Questioning if what we have been taught is love, really is love.

2. Acknowledging that the concept of love we know is not

actually love but rather includes elements such as attachment, expectation, condition, and judgement.

3. Opening the thought process to what it would be like to eliminate the clutter surrounding the emotion we call love. Tasting the beginning of the freedom this brings.

4. Beginning to release conditions on those on the periphery of our existence – casual relationships, acquaintances, and those we interact with in public. This mainly happens as we begin to "catch" our judgemental thoughts.

New constructs that may begin to appear in this phase: "It's okay that she is this way," "That he wants to do such-and-such is a reflection of himself, not of me," "I want what is best for you, and I trust you to know what you need most in this moment."

5. Beginning to release conditions on those more intimate in our lives, who are more inclined to reach our "trigger points." We will create (for our highest and greatest good) situations in which we are given a choice. Do we choose to grow our hearts, or do we choose to restrict our hearts? (There is no stagnation in love; we are continually growing or contracting.)

This includes appreciating "messy" moments as moments of great growth – not as areas for us to judge or criticize - and leads to a similar understanding of "messy" relationships. This phase is when the reality of what it is like to absolutely love begins to form more concretely in our minds. When we meet these challenges and choose to be brave, we truly start to push our limits and grow our hearts in compelling ways.

6. Incorporating these beliefs into love for ourselves. This means forgiving ourselves, releasing past "mistakes," and compliment-ing and loving ourselves as freely as we would a newborn baby.

7. Understanding that the sum of our experiences will never equal the sum of anyone else's experiences and, therefore, acknowledging that only we can make our best determinations. Accompanying this is a true release in judgement of others' choices. This includes an absence of criticism, disdain, pity, moral superiority, righteousness, a need to coddle, etc.

8. Refining these emotions over and over, through our life experiences, relationships, and challenges, and understanding they are there for us to continually expand our concept of love.

Catch These Blocks Before They Grow

Challenge: Sometimes when I mention unconditional love, people react defensively. One reason is a fear of losing control. They are complacent exerting conditions on those they love because it helps them feel they have a semblance of control. Releasing these conditions would create a situation, in their minds, where their carefully crafted worlds might spiral uncontrollably.

Solution: Recognizing that we do not control anyone but ourselves will release this illusion and allow us to embrace the natural flow of life.

Challenge: People also resist unconditional love due to a misinterpretation of its meaning. They sometimes believe loving unconditionally means allowing others to treat them poorly, without any repercussions. Absolutely not! Sometimes our best path is to love someone from a distance. If someone is treating us in a way that doesn't reflect our divine soul, or if we are in a non-supportive environment - then it is part of loving ourselves to break free.

Solution: Setting boundaries for what we choose to have present in our lives will affirm unconditional love for ourselves.

Challenge: We sometimes want to make ourselves right and the other person wrong. But, is that really ever the case? Perhaps that soul accepted the responsibility of making a "mistake" so we could learn from the situation. How many people in our lives do we have a tendency to blame, and how might they have helped us? Consider that our enemies and our victimizers may actually be our greatest saviors.

Solution: Recognizing each moment and each person as a gift toward the evolution of our souls will allow us to understand the lesson in all.

Extending Unconditional Love to Ourselves

The true journey for absolute love must begin and end with ourselves.

Before we can fully love others we must fully love ourselves. For most of us, this involves a back and forth process of growing in self-love, growing in love for others – and then repeating this process many, many times.

Whenever we are experiencing a lack of love that we perceive to be from others, it always stems from some place within us that we are not extending love. When we are full of love for ourselves, no one can take it away. When we are lacking in love for ourselves, we look to others to refill what they cannot.

This is why it is so important to take those situations that feel difficult for us and use them as opportunities to love ourselves more. Certainly, some experiences are easier than others – but this is how we grow in love.

Painful experiences, while difficult, are actually events for which we can be thankful. At their core, they are showing us an area where we can strengthen our internal love.

It's important to remember that no one actually ever does anything to us. People merely act out of themselves and their own reflection of reality.

Strengthening our love for ourselves is essential on the path to true unconditional love. We must ask why we learned to doubt ourselves, why we learned to criticize ourselves, and why we learned to fear. We must also release any judgements we have of others and ourselves for the parts we have played in creating what had been our perception of love – understanding that, for whatever reasons, we needed those experiences.

It is also important to practice transitioning our thinking from that of focusing on what we don't like about ourselves to what we do like about ourselves. This positive mental connection is essential for us to connect with the love we initially felt when our souls were born into physical form here on Earth.

Extending Unconditional Love to Others

When we have caring feelings for others, we want the best for them. The challenge is wanting the best for them, while allowing the reality they choose to create – and allowing it gracefully, peacefully, and with full support.

When it may appear to us that others are making mistakes … we can appreciate that life is offering them growth lessons and applaud them for taking on these challenges.

When we may want to disagree with the lifestyle of others … we can recognize that their souls are in a different – but equally valuable – place as ours and are serving an equally valuable purpose.

When we feel others are causing us harm or pain … we can reevaluate our own boundaries, reinforce our own love, and recognize that everyone's perception of reality is different and that those differences are reflected through our own actions and reactions.

A large part of extending unconditional love to others is releasing attachment. This does not mean we release all intimate relationships – we need those to grow. But, an evaluation of why we feel the need to have a certain outcome or response will bring the issue back to our own selves, where we can work through it with love.

Romantic Relationships

Romantic Relationships offer us the potential to evolve our souls in dramatic and intimate ways. Sometimes these relationships are brief and powerful. Sometimes they are long and quiet but leave an indelible mark on our souls.

When two people come together in lifelong partnership, it is a blessing enabling them to learn and ultimately embody unconditional love. The couple is gifted with a lifetime to honor each other as separate beings and to unite as one.

Each day two people remain in love is a day that love blossoms, not only for themselves but for everyone. For as one loves more, the world loves more. And this is the beauty of love, that it is infinite in abundance.

When we are blessed with romantic relationships of any length or strength, we can choose to recognize what purpose a relationship may be serving for our souls. Once we are able to see a larger purpose, it helps us to release some of the smaller, less loving emotions that may come up over the course of the relationship's growth.

When Unconditional Love Is Not Extended to Us

Most of us have a tendency to default to pain (or anger masking pain) when someone we want to offer us unconditional love does not. There are several factors to consider when this happens.

1. We receive what we offer so it is important to start with this premise first. Who in our lives are we not offering absolute love? What part of ourselves are we not offering absolute love? What area of sensitivity is triggered – and how can we send that area more love?

2. Use moments of pain as moments to be grateful. When an area of sensitivity is brought out by someone else, we can thank them because we are now aware of an area within us that needs more love. When we are fully whole and loving to ourselves, we experience no pain at the hands of others.

For example, if someone were to criticize us in an area we are very secure, what would be our reaction? To laugh, to shrug it off, to forget about it moments later. But, when someone criticizes one of our sensitive areas, what would be our reaction? To sulk, to get angry, to obsess for weeks about the agony of it? We can use those moments as instructional moments and allow them to propel us to greater envelopments of love.

3. Like attracts like. When there are relationships that cause us discomfort because of a continual conditional love, it may be time to shift out of the relationship. Trust that when you are

ready for a higher-love relationship, it will come to you. Also trust that you will remain in a conditional-love relationship as long as you are still learning what you are meant to learn.

When Unconditional Love Is Extended to Us

Some of us may not know the feeling of pure love offered us; some of us may have had only glimpses. Remember or imagine as closely as you can what this feels like – the absolute support, the absolute caring, the feeling of being surrounded and cradled in absolute joy.

This is the state we are seeking to replicate – both toward ourselves and toward others. Taking a few moments each day to reconnect with this feeling will strengthen its presence in our lives and allow us to embrace it deeper and more fully as we travel the moments of our lives.

When unconditional love is extended to us, it is our greatest gift on Earth.

Growing to Embody Unconditional Love

Following you will find "My Philosophy on Unconditional Love," the "Thoughts" and "Affirmations," and the "Love in Action Steps." Please enjoy, embrace, and embody them at your own pace.

Know that you are fully supported, fully loved, and fully accepted for the wondrous being of love you are.

My Philosophy

on

Unconditional Love

xoxoxoxoxoxoxoxoxoxoxoxoxoxoxoxoxoxoxoxoxoxoxoxoxoxoxoxoxo

It is our natural state to give and receive unconditional love.

What we crave most in the world is the conscious knowledge that we are unconditionally loved.

We are able to love unconditionally when we release fears and expectations.

God loves everyone unconditionally.

We erase perceived pain when we are in a state of unconditional love.

Loving ourselves unconditionally is essential for loving others unconditionally.

When we begin to love ourselves unconditionally, we see beautiful transformation in our lives.

I am love.

You are love.

Thoughts,
Affirmations,
and Love in Action Steps

Thoughts from Caroline

Which one of us hasn't been presented by God with a change in "our" plans? And, when it happens, how often is our first reaction one of blame - blame of others, ourselves, bad luck, life? When we choose to see these changes as corrections in our larger life path instead of reasons for blame, we can learn to see their value. What lessons do they bring? What attachment is it in our best interest to release? If we can trust that everything - every single thing in our lives - is present in order to help us, we can grow smoothly and quickly into the beautiful, unconditionally loving nature of our souls.

Affirmation

I am open to life's surprises and view them as opportunities to grow in love.

Love in Action Steps

1. Remember something wonderful about a place or person you've left behind – and thank God for having allowed you the experience.

2. Write a note to your future self about how grateful you are to be living your life.

Thoughts from Caroline

Betrayal. Loss of trust. Trauma of the heart. These are some of the most devastating emotions we can experience. Our world crumbles, and we feel that all we have believed to be true was merely an illusion. These are moments where we face decisions crucial to our growth: Do we allow it to continue? Do we walk away? Or do we forgive or change? It is in that choice that we cement our belief in unconditional love because each path provides growth toward love – for ourselves and for the other.

Affirmation

Loving myself unconditionally will heal my relationships with others.

Love in Action Steps

1. Send loving feelings to someone who has hurt you. Imagine that your souls are at peace with each other.

2. Call the angels to you, and ask them to wrap their wings around you. Allow them to take away your pain. Alternatively, ask the universe to wrap you in white light.

Thoughts from Caroline

Sometimes we are provided an opportunity not only to forgive, but to release – our pain, our resentment, our perceived injustice. It is important in these times to realize that it is our choice. God provides us free will so we can make the best decision we are able to make in that moment. At times, we surprise even ourselves when we take giant leaps forward in our soul's evolution and act more loving than we ever imagined we could. In these moments, unconditional love is a tangible presence and a healer of all.

Affirmation

Love overcomes all.

Love in Action Steps

1. Think of your most difficult situation. Picture life five years from now and how well your higher self navigated you through the present challenges.

2. Release judgement on one "mistake" you have made and one "mistake" someone else has made.

Thoughts from Caroline

Our souls follow their own unique paths. We honor our individual journeys by recognizing that we are not able to choose the actions of another soul. Sometimes our only option in a challenging situation is to send someone unconditional love. The often-unrecognized beauty in these situations, however, is that unconditional love is the greatest gift we can bestow on another. Whatever choices are ultimately made and whatever the outcome, unconditional love blesses the path.

Affirmation

Our individual journeys teach us love.

Love in Action Steps

1. In a public place, seek out someone who seems very different from yourself. Mentally appreciate all the varied qualities this person radiates.

2. Pick one thing that bothers you about someone else, and let it go.

Thoughts from Caroline

The closest vision we have on earth to seeing pure, innocent, unconditional love is in the eyes of a child. Children are a reminder of who we can be and of who we really are. When we are blessed by the presence of children, we have an opportunity to connect with and experience unconditional love in a wondrous way. When we are blessed with the opportunity to raise children, we learn from their reflection of us, and we can reconnect with the pure, innocent part of our own hearts.

Affirmation

Children can be our greatest teachers on the path of love.

Love in Action Steps

1. Look into a child's eyes, and try to communicate a positive emotion without using words.

2. Close your eyes, and use all your senses to bring back the happiest moment of your childhood.

Thoughts from Caroline

To love ourselves unconditionally, we must learn our own strength. Recognizing our own capabilities is the first step toward self-appreciation, which leads to self-approval, self-respect, and – finally – self-love. A sudden shock can propel us forward along the path of unconditional love in ways that no ordinary action could. When this happens, we are wise to appreciate the good it brings into our lives.

Affirmation

All of life's challenges are opportunities to grow in love.

Love in Action Steps

1. Write down ten things you like about your personality and ten things you like about your physical form. Place the lists in front of you, and smile at them for five full minutes.

2. What is one wonderful thing you did today? Tell yourself, "Congratulations!"

Thoughts from Caroline

To choose the path of unconditional love, we must include ourselves in the journey. Setting boundaries that limit behaviors and environments we feel are unhealthy is a step toward valuing the sanctity of our own souls. And, when we release our expectations that someone be a certain way or fill a certain role, we are blessed with the freedom to discover that we hold the very quality we thought we needed someone else to provide.

Affirmation

I offer compassion and set my own boundaries.

Love in Action Steps

1. Say "no" to something or someone when you would have said "yes" only out of obligation.

2. Express a want that you had been afraid or reluctant to express – and stand by it.

Thoughts from Caroline

One of the best gifts we can give ourselves is to listen to our inner guidance. Even though at times our earthly circumstances may seem to have a louder voice, our soul knows what is best overall and what is best for us. When we listen, the beauty of our life's path and purpose is laid out before us, and we are supported in ways we never would have thought possible. Honoring our heart's intent will always bring us to more unconditional love for ourselves and for others.

Affirmation

My passions open doors to love.

Love in Action Steps

1. Imagine that you have no responsibilities or obligations. What would you do with your life? Is there a way to bring an element of that into today?

2. Take a bath by candlelight, and don't get out until your mind is quieter.

Thoughts from Caroline

We've all been in situations where we felt different or "on the outside." Perhaps we looked or acted differently, thought differently, or hid a secret we felt no one would accept. We can choose to absorb pain from these moments, or we can choose to view them in a different way. Imagine for a moment that God wants to strengthen your belief in yourself: Could the universe create circumstances that would enable you to learn that belief? When we are pushed in a direction that is not comfortable for us, we learn to push back with an even greater force. These moments build who we are.

Affirmation

I appreciate differences and embrace similarities as a way to promote love.

Love in Action Steps

1. Liberate yourself by telling someone one secret that you have been afraid to reveal.

2. Write down something "different" about yourself and why you love it.

Thoughts from Caroline

Love is the strongest emotion. Even in the face of unspeakable tragedy, love is greater. When actions occur that seem to challenge our sense of what is good in the world, we have a choice where to put our focus. The knowledge that good can come from all, that good is in all, helps us make that choice. We can always find love and help it grow. We are called to love - it is our home.

Affirmation

Forgiveness is a direct path to unconditional love.

Love in Action Steps

1. Pick any country labeled as "terrorist," and perform an internet search to find someone in that country living a life of love.

2. List five positive things resulting from what you feel is a tragedy.

Thoughts from Caroline

Regret serves no purpose. Action in the present moment does, and it is where we hold the power to put our focus. We are called to embrace each moment and bring it to a greater state of love, with the knowledge that we always do the best we can. Each moment, each challenge, each relationship is an opportunity to open our hearts. Hearts aren't stagnant – they either grow or they constrict. What will you choose for your heart today?

Affirmation

I love unconditionally NOW.

Love in Action Steps

1. Acknowledge one relationship "sticking point" that is ego-based – big or small – and release it.

2. Do something kind today.

Thoughts from Caroline

Often we view love as a "search." We believe we have to go somewhere, do something, be a certain way to find love. What we discover on that external search is that love is inside of us and always has been inside of us. The journey takes us on a path toward our own hearts, where the greatest treasure imaginable resides. Every fiber of our being, down to the smallest particle of our being, is love. We have love. We are love. We provide love for the entire world, simply by existing.

Affirmation

I am love.

Love in Action Steps

1. Look yourself in the mirror, and say, "I love you."

2. Close your eyes, and imagine love radiating from your heart to your household, your city, your country, and your world.

Thoughts from Caroline

We are surrounded by love. At all times, in every moment, love embraces us and envelops us. In our moments of need, we can call on love to support and comfort us. Understanding that love can arrive in infinite forms – from a loved one's guidance to a furry kitten at our doorstep – helps us to recognize its presence in our lives. When we open ourselves to love, it always finds a way.

Affirmation

Love is eternal and all-encompassing.

Love in Action Steps

1. Remember something nice that was done for you.

2. Play with an animal. Allow yourself to be fully engaged with the animal and fully present in the moment.

Thoughts from Caroline

How can we understand the meaning of love, when we have bandied the word about like a ball? By remembering that love, in its essence, is absolute. We can choose to give the word the value it deserves and then act in a way that reflects its meaning. Extending this absolute love to ourselves and to others ensures a peaceful, happy life. We can radiate pure love because we are pure love.

Affirmation

The more I focus my thoughts on love, the more I will be able to act in love.

Love in Action Steps

1. Draw a picture of what love means to you.

2. Release one thought pattern that involves a condition on love.

Thoughts from Caroline

Through the empowerment of ourselves, we are able to empower others. And, through unconditionally loving ourselves, we can unconditionally love others. Trusting that all is right – every situation, every person – frees us from the emotions that can pull us toward negative thoughts and actions. This trust enables us to live in a state of unconditional love.

Affirmation

I choose positive thoughts and emotions.

Love in Action Steps

1. Do something that makes you happy – and catch yourself smiling.

2. Make one choice today that feels empowering.

Thoughts from Caroline

We can erase the words "mistake" and "failure" from our vocabulary. We can choose instead to view every action as an experience for growth. Consequences are corrections, and our next actions can always be influenced by what we have learned. We can choose to grow as quickly as our soul desires by recognizing the lessons that present themselves. We also can choose to release others from our projections and recognize that they, too, are on a path of learning.

Affirmation

Loving myself is the beginning of all the love I can offer.

Love in Action Steps

1. Write down one "mistake" you think you have made, and also write down what you learned from it. Then, burn, bury, or throw away the piece of paper.

2. Recognize one signal the universe is sending you, and endeavor to discover its significance.

Thoughts from Caroline

We can choose to reinforce others' perception of unconditional love by being an example of it. We can also choose to verbalize our unconditional love and support. Encouraging and inspiring another to believe in the possibility of unconditional love reinforces our own belief. Through these types of unconditional relationships, we are provided a safe foundation from which to grow.

Affirmation

I choose to offer unconditional emotional support to myself and others.

Love in Action Steps

1. Surprise someone by verbally releasing a condition you had placed on your love.

2. Go beyond a casual encounter to find out how someone is really doing.

Thoughts from Caroline

What does it take to love? Is it an action we take, or a word we speak, or a thought we think? It can be all of these or any of these. But, love also transcends the usual human experience and envelops the soul. Our soul unconditionally loves. In each and every moment, even when our human form falters, our soul loves. When we are presented an opportunity to experience unconditional love at a soul level, we are truly blessed.

Affirmation

Love transcends my body, as it is the state of my soul.

Love in Action Steps

1. Meditate on an intimate relationship, and speak to the other person's soul.

2. Make one statement aloud today that comes entirely from your heart.

Thoughts from Caroline

Especially as children, we can become conditioned by our environments. Thankfully, we can consciously choose to re-condition ourselves. We are able to do this without harboring resentment or guilt because we appreciate that every so-called negative action directed toward us and from us allows us to experience a new aspect of growth. We can realize that each step we take toward unconditionally loving ourselves builds upon the one before, until one day we realize we have pieced back the fragments of our heart.

Affirmation

I value and love myself.

Love in Action Steps

1. Think of a painful childhood experience, and relive it in your mind in such a way that you are focused on what you are learning in each moment, rather than what you are feeling.

2. Give a meaningful, heartfelt compliment to a child.

Thoughts from Caroline

Animals provide an outlet for us to express love without the fear we might be tempted to allow in with a person. Because we feel completely and unconditionally accepted and loved by them, we can more easily provide them with the same love. We can appreciate their unconditionally giving natures, and, with conscious effort, attempt to emulate them. They help us, and we help them – a beautiful combination and another example for us to follow. Animals can teach us the most wondrous of lessons!

Affirmation

All experiences teach us love.

Love in Action Steps

1. Spend an hour at an animal shelter playing with or walking the animals.

2. Bring a journal to a dog park, and write about how happy the dogs are – simply to be alive.

Thoughts from Caroline

If God deems us worthy of absolute love, who are we to doubt our lovability? If God has deemed our neighbors and our friends and even our enemies as worthy of absolute love, who are we to doubt their lovability? What better example do we have for how to love than God? If we believe God loves us absolutely, then we should choose to love ourselves absolutely. If we believe God loves others absolutely, then we should choose also to love them absolutely. We may want to complicate the matter of love, but God's love is simple, and so can be ours.

Affirmation

I embrace absolute love.

Love in Action Steps

1. Start the morning with the intention of loving everyone with whom you come in contact.

2. When in a public place, such as walking a trail, send love from your heart to every person you pass.

Thoughts from Caroline

Fear is perhaps the greatest obstacle to unconditional love. We can release fears when we understand that love is always greater than any fear. Each time we discover a fear, we can acknowledge it and choose to walk through it. This renders the fear powerless and restores the natural power of our souls. We are also able to step further into the flow of the universe, where we will feel rewarded for our bravery, as the flow of the universe feels safe and peaceful and easy.

Affirmation

Love is always stronger than my fears.

Love in Action Steps

1. The next time you are afraid emotionally, instead of over-thinking it, step through it.

2. Ask your angels to help you through one of your fears.

Thoughts from Caroline

Family bonds often provide our strongest examples of unconditional love. When we are blessed with this in our lives, it gives us confidence in our own pursuits and the ability to pass this example of unconditional love on to further generations. Even through difficult times, the underlying love remains, and we can always choose to focus on the strengths of the unconditional love we have received and given.

Affirmation

I choose to see my family relationships as opportunities to create love.

Love in Action Steps

1. Call someone in your family just to say, "Hello."

2. Thank a parent, relative, or mentor for a lesson they taught you as a child.

Thoughts from Caroline

Our thoughts about ourselves control the reality we experience and color everything we see, hear, and feel. We can choose positive thoughts, we can choose supportive thoughts, and we can choose loving thoughts. Recognizing the sanctity of our soul helps. Recognizing we wouldn't criticize a friend the way we criticize ourselves helps. Recognizing that the approval we most need in the world is our own is life-changing.

Affirmation

I deserve my own love.

Love in Action Steps

1. While getting ready in the morning, compliment everything about yourself.

2. In your home or office, add a picture or handmade decoration or collage that makes you feel good.

Thoughts from Caroline

No matter how much pain we have experienced in our lives, we can choose to release it. No matter what wrongs we have perceived ourselves to have committed, we can choose to release them. We can choose to release all illusions that we are anything less than a perfect soul from God. If we reach a dark night of our soul, we can rejoice, for we know the dawn will bring with it a promise of rebirth. All is well in God's world.

Affirmation

I release my chains of bondage and find peace in my own heart.

Love in Action Steps

1. Take ten minutes to imagine you have never experienced pain.

2. The next time you wake up in the middle of the night – worried or hurting – remember that God loves you.

Thoughts from Caroline

How many times have we claimed to love God unconditionally and then stood by as a neighbor struggled, or as a friend spiraled, or even distanced ourselves when a relative simply "got on our nerves?" We cannot love God unconditionally without loving everyone and everything unconditionally. We are all part of the same spiritual family, even those on the other side of the world whom we will never meet. Recognizing that we are all parts of a whole, and that we, ourselves, are a valued part of that whole, will reunite us together as one.

Affirmation

I focus on extending unconditional love to all, including those who are hardest for me.

Love in Action Steps

1. Call or start a conversation with a friend, relative, or acquaintance you have been avoiding.

2. To someone you will never meet – send a care package, say something complimentary or appreciative via the internet, or otherwise impact someone in a positive way.

Thoughts from Caroline

Trust. Perhaps we trust that we will be able to arrive at work that day, or that the market will have a loaf of bread we can purchase – but how deeply do we trust? Do we believe God is always there for us? Do we believe we will be provided for in a time of need? Do we believe we are always loved? And always loveable? Allowing in the mighty belief that we are always okay, in every moment, and that all is as it should be brings us an immeasurable peace and allows us the freedom to fully embrace each experience that comes into our lives.

Affirmation

I am loveable, as I am.

Love in Action Steps

1. Pick one upcoming conversation, meeting, or event, and say to the universe: I trust that everything will be okay.

2. Do something out of your comfort zone.

Thoughts from Caroline

Imagine for a moment that every person on the planet followed his or her passion. That every one of us woke up thankful to participate in the day's activities. Imagine the inspiration and sheer joy humanity would experience. Imagine not simply "making it through the day," but, rather, using divine sparks of inspiration to improve our existence. Imagine rejoicing at the infinite opportunities we have. Imagine grasping that our life is a matter of our own creating. We can imagine all this – and we can become it.

Affirmation

I value my passion and trust my feelings.

Love in Action Steps

1. Draw or make a collage of all you love in life.

2. Start your day with the intent of loving the work you perform.

Thoughts from Caroline

Inside all of us, there is a yearning. A yearning to be understood and accepted and loved on all levels. We will reach a day when this unconditional love is given and received by everyone. For now, we are able to learn it through divine relationships. A precious gift, these relationships can help us evolve rapidly and in ways beyond what we are able to do on our own. What a blessing when we choose to be open to them!

Affirmation

I embrace spiritual relationships as opportunities to grow exponentially in love.

Love in Action Steps

1. Whether single or attached, meditate on your life partner or a soul mate, imagining that you are flying together above the earth, holding hands.

2. When given a chance to welcome a new spiritual relationship or to evolve an ongoing one – embrace it.

Thoughts from Caroline

What blame are we holding that keeps us from moving forward? When we understand that acceptance and contentment are within us at all times, it allows us to re-frame the experiences we feel have caused us harm. What are we able to learn from the situation or from the person? What value can be found? And, what are we holding against someone, in this moment, that we can release?

Affirmation

I release judgements of myself and others, trusting we are all on our best path.

Love in Action Steps

1. Take a bath or shower, and picture all your judgements of yourself going down the drain.

2. Burn incense, while allowing your blame of someone else to drift away with the smoke.

Thoughts from Caroline

In a world full of love, it is up to us to choose to recognize that love. We can enlarge our scope of vision beyond our pursuits and goals and perceived complications to allow love to enter. When we wonder, "What is the point of our existence?" the answer always comes down to love. We are rewarded with a richer, fuller existence when we remember love and when we embrace it in all its forms.

Affirmation

I choose to allow love into my life.

Love in Action Steps

1. Find a way to put love into a regular, everyday action.

2. Accept help the next time it is offered.

Thoughts from Caroline

What communications are we missing? Are we allowing the voices of animals or our angels to reach us? Are we too busy to hear the voice of God? We can benefit from opening our perception to the messages that are all around us. Look into the eyes of a dolphin, and you will recognize each other. Smell the scent of a flower, and you will sense the presence of God. Nature presents us with so many gifts; it is up to us to choose to see them.

Affirmation

I see beauty and love in all life forms.

Love in Action Steps

1. Take a walk in nature with no electronic gadgets, and use all of your senses to fully embrace your surroundings.

2. Pick flowers that others might consider weeds, and put them in a pretty vase.

Thoughts from Caroline

We all have personas we embrace. Sometimes we are a business executive or a mother or a volunteer. But, in every moment, we are more than any persona or any label. We have a divine soul at our core, and that soul is at all times capable of reaching out to another soul. We always have an option to send unconditional love to the world. There is no moment, ever, when we cannot send our love to someone or something. We always have the power to heal.

Affirmation

We always can find ways to love.

Love in Action Steps

1. Reach out to someone who appears stressed.

2. Say hello and smile to a stranger who is not already smiling.

Thoughts from Caroline

Harboring guilt is one of our most destructive tendencies. When we are able to understand that everything happens for a reason, we can then validate its gift to our lives. And, from that validation, we can act. We can share our knowledge with others, and we can spread the lesson we have learned. All has reason. Nothing is ever in vain. We can be thankful we are blessed with the ability to share with others our newfound knowledge.

Affirmation

We are all loved, and we all can love.

Love in Action Steps

1. Catch thoughts of guilt, and shoo them away with a mental feather duster.

2. Share something you've learned about life with another person or with a group.

Thoughts from Caroline

Perhaps the most profound element of unconditional love is the development of unconditional love for ourselves. We may think, "Who am I to be proud of my accomplishments when others have done more?" Or, "Who am I to enjoy an expensive meal when so many others are starving?" We can even convince ourselves, "I am not valuable enough" to take care of my body, or put my needs first, or take a needed time-out. God didn't make just some souls valuable and loveable – we are all in His image. It is essential we honor God's wisdom and learn to value and love ourselves.

Affirmation

I deserve unconditional love as I am, now.

Love in Action Steps

1. Pamper yourself with a treat, and relish every moment.

2. Accept your success, and value it.

Thoughts from Caroline

Each moment presents an opportunity to experience unconditional love. Even a seemingly mundane encounter can have profound significance when we step outside of our boxes and see the encounter as one between souls. What message would our soul choose to offer? What might we learn from this person, who, from a human perspective, may be judged as having little to offer? It is up to us to capture the importance of each moment and allow our souls to heal each other.

Affirmation

I recognize the potential for love in each moment.

Love in Action Steps

1. Be forgiving and nice to every driver you encounter on the road today.

2. Genuinely compliment your waiter, checker, taxi driver, etc.

Thoughts from Caroline

When we are called to be a support system for someone, the greatest gift we can provide them is unconditional space – a space where we are not offended, a space where we do not ignite further controversy, a space where we do not act as an injured party, a space where we do not encourage their guilt for certain behaviors. In a challenging situation with another, we can put aside our ego and meet them with our soul. We can choose to provide them the room they need to grow.

Affirmation

I exercise patience with myself and others in my pursuit of unconditional love.

Love in Action Steps

1. Let someone close to you have a "messy moment" without judging it or taking it personally.

2. Listen with your heart.

Closing Thoughts

Let us take a moment to imagine love. Let us feel love – the love we have for others, the love we have for ourselves, the love we have for the world. Let us allow love to envelop us. Let us now send out these feelings of love. Let us shower the world with every thought and every experience we know of love. Let us imagine lovers blissful in their union. Let us be love, and let us see others as love.

In this, we recognize we are one. One in a search for the truthfulness of our souls, one in a search for a return to love. As we embrace absolute love, we return to our natural state of unconditional love. Our pursuit of pure love becomes pure love.

Know that I love you and I love with you, for we all become love as you become love. I celebrate my oneness with you and bless you with the ultimate gift of absolute love.

The "Love Like God" series is guiding you to rethink and redefine the love in your life. This is good. Begin here. You have discovered a starting point to a life filled with love that is true, love that is unconditional. Embrace it in all its joy and freedom, and celebrate this return to the pureness of your heart!

Remember:
All is love.
You are loved.
I love you.

Please share this message and the "Love Like God" books with others.

Blessings,
Caroline A. Shearer

Quotes to Inspire Unconditional Love

"Even after all this time, the sun never says to the earth, 'You owe me.' Look what happens with a love like that. It lights the whole sky." ~ Hafez of Shiraz

"Where you find no love, put love -- and you will find love." ~ John of the Cross.

"Love is life. All, everything that I understand, I understand only because I love. Everything is, everything exists, only because I love. Everything is united by it alone." ~ Leo Tolstoy

"To love for the sake of being loved is human, but to love for the sake of loving is angelic." ~ Alphonse de Lamartine

"The beginning of love is to let those we love be perfectly themselves, and not to twist them to fit our own image. Otherwise, we love only the reflection of ourselves we find in them." ~ Thomas Merton

"You, yourself, as much as anybody in the entire universe, deserve your love and affection." ~ Buddha

Mother Teresa

"I have found the paradox, that if you love until it hurts, there can be no more hurt, only more love."

"The success of love is in the loving - it is not in the result of loving. Of course it is natural in love to want the best for the other person, but whether it turns out that way or not does not determine the value of what we have done."

"If you judge people, you have no time to love them."

"Intense love does not measure, it just gives."

About Absolute Love Publishing

Absolute Love Publishing is an independent, specialty publisher founded on spiritual principles. Our mission is to create and publish projects promoting goodness in the world. We are based in Austin, Texas, USA. We also are home to the imprint Spirited Press, an assisted-publishing platform, with full-service publishing and a la carte editing, marketing, and publishing services. Absolute Love Publishing owns min-e-book.com and the trademark, min-e-book™. A min-e-book™ is a shorter-style e-book designed for a quick read.

About Caroline A. Shearer

Caroline A. Shearer is a bestselling author, speaker, and the founder of Absolute Love Publishing. Her popular books include "Dead End Date," the first book in the Adventures of a Lightworker series; "Love Like God: Embracing Unconditional Love;" and the min-e-book™ "Raise Your Vibration: Tips and Tools for a High-Frequency Life." Known as a fresh, distinctive, spiritual voice, Caroline's vision is to promote goodness and love in the world through the inspiration of others.

Who Am I?

I am a student of unconditional love. Elements in my life have prompted me to explore the meaning of love and have brought me to a point where I see it, or its potential, everywhere. I am learning to remember my true nature, which is to love myself and others absolutely.

I could instantaneously allow this to happen – that possibility exists for all of us – but, like most, I have my own journey and make strides in my own time. For now, I embrace those moments of total freedom when I release my fears and my attachments and allow myself to feel the blissful love inside my heart.

If we all chose to define our thoughts and actions by the principle of love, what would result, but even more love?

I do believe all we need is love. And, we will get there through an awareness of the power and beauty of that love.